Faith That Will Work for You

—

by
Charles Capps

Unless otherwise indicated, all Scripture quotations are taken from the King James Version of the Bible.

Some Scripture quotations marked (Berry) are taken from the Interlinear Greek-English New Testament with a Greek-English Lexicon and New Testament Synonyms by George Ricker Berry: Copyright © 1987 by Hines & Noble. Reprinted by Baker Book House, Grand Rapids, Michigan.

Printed 2016

Faith That Will Work for You
ISBN 13: 978-0-9618975-7-4
Formerly titled, *How to Have Faith in Your Faith*
ISBN 10: 0-89274-415-4
Copyright © 1999 by Charles Capps
P.O. Box 69
England, Arkansas 72046

Published by CAPPS PUBLISHING
P.O. Box 69
England, AR 72046

Contents

1

Back to Basics

There are some basic things about faith that we need to continually go over. Just because we have heard it once doesn't necessarily mean we know it.

Sometimes it is good to go back and review some old truths from God's Word that have become old hat, so to speak. Before you realize it, you have forgotten some things that you knew years ago.

Some of these basics are found in Hebrews 11:1.

> Now faith is the substance of things hoped for, the evidence of things not seen.

Notice this sentence: Now faith is.... Even though the word *now* in the context is not used in this sense, allow me to direct your thought to this word as though it were referring to present tense for the purpose of revealing something about faith that is important to all of us.

Now faith is.... Faith that is the substance of things hoped for is always *now* faith. The substance of things hoped for is always *now*.

You can say it several different ways. If faith is not *now*, it's not faith. If it's not faith that is present tense, it's not the substance of things hoped for.

Believe When You Pray

Sometimes people keep putting off things God promised until some later date. But Jesus taught, ...What things soever ye desire, when ye pray, believe that ye receive them, and ye shall have them (Mark 11:24).

When are you going to believe you receive what you ask in prayer—when you receive the answer or when you pray? You should believe you receive *when you pray*.

If you pray this afternoon at three o'clock, it will be *now* when you pray.

Let's say it this way: Now faith is, or faith is now.

Let me say again that even though the intent of the word *now* in Hebrews 11:1 is not used as a present-tense word, let's use it that way to provoke your thinking. Let's think of the words on both sides of the word *faith* as being present-tense words: *Now* faith *is.*

Notice Hebrews 11:6:

> But without faith it is impossible to please him: for he that cometh to God must believe that he is, and that he is a rewarder of them that diligently seek him.

Note the phrase, that he is. It's present tense. It doesn't just mean believing that there is a God, but believing that He is in the now.

Your faith has to be in the *now,* in the present tense. It can't be put off into the future or back into the past. It must be present, abiding—faith that is now.

Faith that *is* in the now is the substance of things.

But you hear so many say, "I believe God's going to do it sometime." That's out in the future.

Make a decision to release faith that is in the now.

If you have the faith, then you have the *substance of things* desired. You have the substance of it, but you don't physically have the thing desired. It has not been manifested. You can't wear it, drive it, or fly it. *But you have the substance of it.* The faith substance is the raw material which will cause the manifestation of the thing desired.

Without this faith, it is impossible to please God, for he that comes to God must believe that He is and that He is the rewarder of them that diligently seek Him.

Yes, faith is the substance of things hoped for, the evidence of things not seen. But what things is faith the substance of? *All the things that God has given us by promise.*

Let's go to 2 Peter, chapter 1, for some insight into these promises.

Simon Peter, a servant and an apostle of Jesus Christ, to them that have obtained like precious faith with us through the righteousness of God and our Saviour Jesus Christ.

—2 Peter 1:1

Who is Peter writing to?

...to them that have obtained like precious faith....

In other words, if you have obtained the same faith in Jesus Christ that these men had, then Peter is writing to you. It doesn't matter what century people are living in. It still applies to those of like faith.

God's Willingness Multiplied

Grace and peace be multiplied unto you through the knowledge of God, and of Jesus our Lord.

—2 Peter 1:2

Grace and peace are not *added* to you, but *multiplied* to you.

Allow me to share with you the definition of grace which the Holy Spirit gave me. He said, *"Grace is God's willingness to use His power and His ability on your behalf, even though you don't deserve it."*

Grace is God's willingness. What a powerful statement!

Most people don't have any trouble believing that God is able to do anything, but they aren't sure He is *willing* to do it for them. They are strong in believing in God's ability but weak in believing in His willingness.

God's willingness is multiplied to you through the knowledge of God and of Jesus our Lord.

The Bible teaches that faith comes by hearing and hearing by the Word of God. Faith in God and His Word comes by hearing what God said.

When you gain the knowledge of God, you gain faith in God. Then you know how God will respond to your faith in Him.

If God's Word is in you, then faith is in you because His Word is filled with faith.

God didn't give Oral Roberts more faith than He gave you. He didn't give Kenneth Hagin more faith than He gave you. These men have the same Bible you have. Your Bible has the same word of faith in it. But your faith must be developed. Faith grows when you plant it.

There are so many who think everyone else was given more faith than they were. But we were all given the same amount. Romans 12:3 says God has dealt to *every* man the measure of faith. Every person was given the same measure. God didn't give one person more than He gave another.

How To Measure Faith

The only way to measure faith is to measure the Word in you because God's Word is filled with faith. If His Word is in you, you have faith.

God gave everyone the whole Word of God in Bible form. The whole Word, or *logos,* is the measure of faith He gave. It contains all the faith that is available in promise form. Some receive it; some don't. God gave everyone the same measure of faith, but it is often rejected.

Faith That Will Work for You

God's willingness to use His power and ability on your behalf is multiplied to you when you gain the knowledge of God. That's the reason some people get more from God than others.

Then some say, "Well, I don't understand why God did that for So-and-so. He never does anything like that for me!

Listen to their words: *"God never does anything like that for me."*

Isn't that amazing? For twenty years they have been saying, "God never does it for me." Jesus said, *"If you believe and doubt not in your heart, the things which you say shall come to pass."* They say those things because they don't have faith in their faith. They have not become personally acquainted with God and His ways through His Word. They don't realize that God is willing; therefore, they have no faith in the Word that is in them.

Faith is in you if the Word of God is in you. But that doesn't necessarily mean that if you've memorized the Bible, you have great faith. You could memorize the Bible and not have an ounce of faith that the promises are yours.

Faith comes by hearing the Word of God. Just because you've *memorized* something doesn't mean you've *heard* it. Years ago I memorized several chapters in the Bible and could quote them, but I had no idea what they meant. All I knew was I could quote them. It produced no faith, for I had not really heard (or received) it in my heart.

But when the Word of God became a part of me, I quit trying to memorize scriptures. I just began to speak and hear the Word. Then the Holy Spirit brought revelation to my spirit.

There is nothing wrong with memorizing scriptures, but just because you have it in your head doesn't mean it's in your heart. When it becomes a part of you, it is a revelation in your spirit. Then God's grace is multiplied to you through the knowledge of God.

God Has Given Us All Things

According as his divine power hath given unto us all things that pertain unto life and godliness, through the

knowledge of him that hath called us
to glory and virtue.

—2 Peter 1:3

This is the way God has given you *all things*
that pertain to life and godliness.

Notice this verse says *God has already
given to us,* not going to one of these days. He
has already done it. He is not going to do any
more about it. He has done all He's ever going
to do about your finances or about your physical health.

You may be thinking, "Do you mean that
I'm going to be this way all my life?" No. I didn't
say that. I said God has done all He is going to
do about it.

Jesus has already provided all these
things. They are already in store for you. They
belong to you. It's just a matter of you tapping
into what God has already given. He doesn't
have to do one more thing for you. He has
given you His faith in His Word, and that faith is
the evidence of things *not seen,* not the
evidence of things you can see.

Believing Is Seeing

So many people say, "I'll believe it when I see it" Someone said, "Seeing is believing." A more scriptural statement would be, *Believing is seeing.* When you believe, you see it in your spirit. You get an image of it on the inside of you. That image controls what you speak and what you do. You see it in your spirit. You *know* it. You know that you know that you know. You don't know how you know, *but you know!*

Once you reach that level of knowing, they can't beat it out of you with a ball bat. It has gotten down on the inside of you. It has become a part of you. You have become one with God's Word.

That oneness is caused by faith, and it is the substance of things that God has already provided you; namely, *all things that pertain to life and godliness.*

2

Partaker of Divine Nature

According as his divine power hath given unto us all things that pertain unto life and godliness, through the knowledge of him that hath called us to glory and virtue:

Whereby are given unto us exceeding great and precious promises: that by these ye might be partakers of the divine nature, having escaped the corruption that is in the world through lust.

—2 Peter 1:3-4

You can be a partaker of the divine nature. There are some people who say, "You must think you're God, saying all these things. Don't you know that God is sovereign?"

Yes, I know God is sovereign. He is sovereign according to His sovereign Word. He said, "I'll not alter the things that come out of My mouth."

I don't care what unbelief comes out of you. God won't alter what He has said. He said what He meant, and He meant what He said. He will not break His Word.

God has given unto us exceeding great and precious promises: that by these ye might be partakers of the divine nature. Notice it says you *might* be (not *would* be) partakers of the divine nature. You have to make a decision to be a partaker of His nature.

Why should people get concerned when we act like God acts and talk like God talks? They should be concerned when we don't act like God would act. If we are sons of God, we should act like our Father God.

God wants us to talk like Him. He wants us to act like Him—*not to be God, but be like God*—because we are created in His image and in His likeness.

But many people will get offended at you and say, "Who do you think you are?"

When they do, just answer, "I'm a partaker of the divine nature. I'm not going to hang around with the old crowd and wallow in unbelief just because someone else does."

Joint-Heirs Can Be Partakers

No, I'm not God, but I'm a son of God. I'm a joint-heir with Jesus and a partaker of the divine nature.

Just because others are not partakers of the divine nature of God is no reason we shouldn't be.

If faith is the substance of things hoped for and the evidence of things not seen, that means *it's the proof of things not seen.* You go to a court of law and say, "I have proof of this thing." If you have proof, then it has to exist or you couldn't have proof of it.

Existence Is Proven by Faith

All these things that God promised already exist in the realm of the spirit, or else faith couldn't be the evidence (or proof) of it. If you believe it, you have the evidence needed. It's in existence the instant you believe it, although you may not physically have it.

But if you keep putting it off, saying, "I believe somewhere, somehow, sometime God is going to do it," it will never come to pass. That is too vague. There is no place established, no time and no way.

Suppose I came to your town, called you on the phone, and said, "I'm in town. We need to get together."

You say, "Okay. That would be good. When?"

"Oh, sometime!"

You ask, "Where?"

I say, "Oh, somewhere," then hang up the phone.

How long do you think it would take for us to get together? We never would get together under those circumstances! We haven't established a place or a time, so we may never meet.

So it is with the things that God has provided. You may never be a partaker unless you establish a time and a place when you believe you receive the promise. It's already provided. God's not going to alter what He has promised.

The Apostle Paul said it like this:

> But as God is true, our word toward you was not yea and nay.
>
> For the Son of God, Jesus Christ, who was preached among you by us, even by me and Silvanus and Timotheus, was not yea and nay, but in him was yea.
>
> For all the promises of God in him are yea, and in him Amen, unto the glory of God by us.
>
> —2 Corinthians 1:18-20

Paul didn't preach a negative gospel, *for all the promises of God in him are yea, and in him Amen.*

What does that mean? God has already said yes to His promises before you ask Him. You already have His will concerning the matter before you ask.

If God promised it, He will stand behind His Word. He won't alter His promise. It doesn't matter if it's in this century or the next. God's Word is eternal. It never is outdated.

3

Fear Is Faith
in Reverse

Faith is the substance of things desired. There is power in faith, in believing. Jesus told the centurion, ...Go thy way; and as thou hast believed, so be it done unto thee (Matt. 8:13).

Believing is not something you always like to do, or always feel like doing. It's a decision you make.

Just as faith is a powerful force, there is also a force opposed to faith called fear. Fear is the reverse gear of faith. It is actually faith in the devil.

If faith is the substance of things desired, then *fear is the substance of things not desired.*

The reason you fear a thing is because you believe in its manifestation. That's why you worry.

You believe in the manifestation of the thing you worry about; otherwise, you wouldn't worry.

Fear Draws Trouble

If you don't control fear or stop it, it will bring the very thing that you don't desire.

Job is a classic example of this.

For the thing which I greatly feared is come upon me, and that which I was afraid of is come unto me.

I was not in safety, neither had I rest, neither was I quiet; yet trouble came.

—Job 3:25-26

Job practiced his fear and greatly feared. Though he was in safety, he didn't know it. The very accusation that Satan brought against God was: "You've hedged him about on every side, and I can't get to him." I can just see God standing there, grinning, saying, *"Yes, I did."*

God said to Satan, "Have you observed My servant, Job?" or "Have you set your eye on My servant, Job?"

Satan had set his eye on Job. God didn't say, "I'm just going to turn him over to you." Satan made a request. Although God didn't honor that request, He did say, "He's in your power." (The footnote says *in your hands*.)

God said, "He *is* in your hands." God didn't put Job there; he was already in the power of the devil because of fear. Fear will also tear *your* hedge down.

Growing Fear Nullifies Faith

Job said, "The thing I've greatly feared has come upon me." There is no doubt that Job had faith, but he lost *faith in his faith*.

You need to know *how to have faith in your faith*.

When you speak your fears, they will grow and nullify your faith. You can't keep the devil from bringing thoughts of doubt and fear to your mind, but those things will die unborn if you don't speak them.

Don't be overcome with evil, but overcome evil with good. Your words give the enemy the license to operate. You give either God or the devil the authority to operate by your words. Your words can give God the ability to move in on your situation in life.

Since faith is the substance of things desired, it seems that fear is the substance of things not desired. So when you talk fear, doubt, and unbelief, you are speaking into existence things you don't desire. When you first say them, you may not realize the power of your words. But the more you speak it, the more it grips you—the more that force multiplies in you. Just as faith comes by hearing, fear comes by hearing.

Jesus said in Matthew 12, verse 35:

> A good man out of the good treasure (or deposit) of the heart bringeth forth good things: and an evil man out of the evil treasure bringeth forth evil things.

Evil Report or Good Report

God calls an evil report anything that doesn't agree with His Word. You can read it in the Book of Numbers, chapter 13. The ten spies brought back an evil report.

The report they brought back was what they saw, what they felt, and what they heard. That's not always an evil report; it depends on what God said about it. The only reason that was considered an evil report was because God said the exact opposite.

Any time you speak contrary to the Word of God, you have spoken an evil report. That doesn't necessarily mean that a man has to be wicked or evil to do that. He could be a deceived Christian. Jesus is saying it's a two-way street.

Whatever is deposited in your heart will produce. Whether it's good or evil, it will come out of your mouth and it will produce after its kind.

You may start saying it and not even believe it. But if you continue to say it, you will eventually believe it because faith comes by hearing.

In Romans 10:17 Paul is speaking specifically of faith in God and in His Word. Faith in God and His Word comes by hearing the Word of God. The opposite of that would be: *Faith in the devil comes by hearing the words of the devil and then quoting the words of the devil.*

Faith in the devil is perverted faith, which we call fear.

Shield of Faith or Doubt

The Apostle Paul said:

> Above all, taking the shield of faith, wherewith ye shall be able to quench all the fiery darts of the wicked.
>
> —Ephesians 6:16

You are able to do it. The opposite end of that truth is that you can take the shield of *doubt* and quench all the *blessings of God*.

So it is a fact from God's Word that the shield of faith can quench *all* that the enemy brings against you. It must be true, then, that you can't take the shield of doubt and quench all the blessings of God—and many have.

What they are saying is producing fear. Their own words are producing the very thing which they are speaking.

I had always thought that the shield of faith was just a figure of speech; but as I was praying in the spirit one day, the Spirit of God said this to me: *"The words you speak produce the shield around you, whether it is faith or fear."* Then I understood that the shield of faith was like a spiritual Plexiglas canopy that encircles an individual and moves with him to quench all the fiery darts of the wicked one.

You build and strengthen that shield, or you weaken it, by the words you speak. If you speak fear, it insulates you and stops the blessings. Fear-filled words will produce more fear, which invites the devil and quenches the blessings of God.

Sometimes people say, "I don't understand these people going around saying their needs are met according to His riches in glory, saying they have abundance and no lack, when I know for a fact that the rent's due and they don't have the money. I believe they're just lying."

No, they are speaking their faith. (2 Cor. 4:13.) If you have been obedient to the Word of God, and you've given, the Bible says it is given to you—good measure, pressed down, shaken together, and running over. That's not talking about what God gives to you. It's talking about you having favor with men. It says, "Men shall give unto you."

If you go to buy a car, the dealer will give you the best deal in town and not know why he did it. But the Word says, ...he which soweth bountifully shall reap also bountifully (2 Cor. 9:6).

By speaking the promise out of your mouth, you implant that promise within your spirit. It becomes a part of you.

There are so many Christians who know the Word, but don't have any faith in their faith. They always want someone to pray the prayer of faith for them.

I believe one of the keys to having faith in your faith is *confessing God's Word until it becomes a part of you.* The words that come out of your mouth have more effect on your spirit than the words of others.

Faith Is the Victory

Faith in God's Word comes by hearing yourself speak what God said. Faith in the devil comes by hearing yourself speak what the devil said.

The Apostle John wrote:

> For whatsoever is born of God overcometh the world: and this is the victory that overcometh the world, even our faith.

> —1 John 5:4

If faith is the victory that overcomes the world, then victory comes through faith in the Word of God which *abides* in you.

When the Word of God abides in you, you have faith. I'm not referring to head faith; I'm referring to heart faith. When the Word becomes a part of you, every time lack shows its head, the first thing out of your mouth should be, "There is abundance, and my God has met my need according to His riches in glory by Christ Jesus."

You should resist pain in your body when it first starts. Resist it the way you resist the devil. That is with the Word of God.

Remember, faith is the victory. But just because you have faith does not necessarily mean you are going to operate in that faith. It could be in you and be dormant or passive. You must have enough faith in your faith to act on it.

So many people have faith in someone else's faith. They always want others to pray the prayer of faith for them, and they never develop faith in their own prayers.

You had to have faith to be born again. The Word of God was the source of that faith. God gave you the Word; you received it as truth and acted accordingly. Salvation was the result of your faith in action.

But faith won't do anything for you if you don't put action to it. A person can go to a grocery store with $1,000 in his billfold. The money is the substance of the things he hopes for. But if he is not *willing to release some of it,* he won't be taking any groceries home. He must leave part of his money if he is going to take the goods. Faith is the ability to get the goods, but the substance must be released.

Through faith in God's Word and acting on what we believe, we overcome. Faith in God causes the Greater One (Jesus) to live big in us.

Ye are of God, little children, and have overcome them: because greater is he that is in you, than he that is in the world.

—1 John 4:4

This is saying we have overcome the Antichrist, the world, the flesh, and the devil because the Greater One is in us.

Speaking God's Word after Him will cause you to have *faith in His Word*. Speaking the promise as though it were already yours will cause you to have *faith in the faith you received from the Word*.

4

Forgiving by Faith

Take heed to yourselves: If thy brother trespass against thee, rebuke him, and if he repent, forgive him.

And if he trespass against thee seven times in a day, and seven times in a day turn again to thee, saying I repent: thou shalt forgive him.

And the apostles said unto the Lord, Increase our faith.

And the Lord said, If ye had faith as a grain of mustard seed, ye might say unto this sycamine tree, Be thou plucked up by the root, and be thou planted in the sea, and it should obey you.

—Luke 17:3-6

If you are having trouble forgiving others, you will have to draw from your faith. *You can forgive others by faith.* Jesus said offenses will come, but you must forgive. If he trespass against thee seven times in a day, and seven times in a day turn again to thee, saying I repent: thou shalt forgive him.

When Jesus talks about forgiving people, the first thing the apostles say is, "Lord, give us more faith." It takes faith to forgive. That's why some people never forgive. They haven't realized that they have to draw from their faith to do it. You have to do some things by faith. ...The just shall live by faith (Rom. 1:17).

Forgiving Is a Decision

You may ask, "How could I forgive by faith when I don't feel like forgiving? I don't even want to forgive them."

Here's how: Start saying, "I make a decision to forgive them, in the name of the Lord Jesus. Because God has forgiven me, I will forgive them. I'm saying in the name of Jesus: I don't hold grudges. I'm saying it: I forgive them in Jesus' name. I'm doing it supernaturally. I'm doing it by faith."

If you keep speaking those words, faith will come and you will forgive them.

The apostles realized that it took faith to forgive. Allow me to paraphrase what they said: "Lord, give us more faith. If someone does us wrong seven times in one day, and we have to forgive him, we will need more faith."

If you continue to draw from your faith without making a deposit, you're going to be overdrawn before long. That's why it's necessary for you to feed upon the Word of God and to keep confessing His Word with your mouth. Remember, faith cometh by hearing.

It's like your bank account. If you keep drawing out of it without depositing anything, after awhile you will show a deficit.

Forgiving requires faith. God says, "Be perfect even as your heavenly Father is perfect." You can do it by faith. You can't be perfect by natural means, but you can by the supernatural.

Faith in the Seed

When the apostles said, "Lord, increase our faith," the Lord said, "If you had faith as a seed...." Forget about the word *mustard*. We have become so involved with the word *mustard* that we have missed the whole point. I heard one fellow say, "If I could just figure out what size the mustard seed faith is..." Well, he missed the whole point.

If Jesus had been in England, Arkansas, He would have said, "If you had faith as a cotton seed..." We know something about cotton seed; we don't know anything about mustard seed.

Jesus was not talking about the size of the seed. He said, "If you had faith **as a seed...**" He's telling you that faith works like a seed. The reason some people can't forgive is because they have never sown that seed. You sow it by saying, "I do forgive them in the name of Jesus." If that continues to come out of your mouth, it will get into your heart and change it.

Many of you have punished your children because you said, "You do that one more time and I'm going to punish you." Later you wished you hadn't said it; but because you said it, you did it. You did it to make your word good.

We're made that way. God knows that, and He's trying to tell you how to get your faith to work to forgive people. You would think the apostles knew everything, wouldn't you? But they didn't, and that's where we missed it, when we thought they knew everything. They had to learn just as we do.

Their Answer

The apostles said, "Lord, increase our faith."

And the Lord said, If ye had faith as a grain of mustard seed, ye might say unto this sycamine tree, Be thou plucked up by the root, and be thou planted in the sea; and it should obey you (Luke 17:6).

The *Interlinear Greek New Testament* says, "You *would* say, and it would obey you" (Berry).

But what's the sycamine tree have to do with it? Not a thing in the world.

I believe they were walking down the road, and there was a tree in the path. Jesus said, "Now, fellows, you don't need more faith, but you need to plant what faith you have. If you had faith as a seed, you would say to this

39

obstacle that's in your path, 'Be plucked up by the roots and be planted in the sea,' and it would obey you."

What would the tree obey? Your faith-filled words.

Faith Secrets Revealed

Here Jesus tells us some great faith secrets. First, faith works as a seed. *Faith as a seed* means faith you are willing to plant. There are some who have faith; but they're not willing to plant it, so they don't have *faith as a seed*. That means they have faith, but not enough faith in that faith to speak it or act on it.

If you had one grain of wheat, what could you do with it? You couldn't make biscuits with it; there wouldn't be enough. The best use of that seed would be to plant it.

If you are smart enough to plant it, the next year you will have much more. *Faith as a seed* has the ability to multiply, but it must first be planted by speaking it.

"If you had faith as a seed, you would say..." What is Jesus talking about? *Forgiveness*. He was talking about forgiving seven times in a day. Unforgiveness is an obstacle to many. The obstacle could be any number of things, such as a financial matter, so don't zero in on just one particular thing. Understand the principle that is involved in removing the obstacles of life.

"If you had faith as a seed, you would say, 'You're not going to stand in my way. You will not hinder me any longer.'"

Unforgiveness Is a Thief of Faith

Talk to unforgiveness. Say, "Unforgiveness, you have to leave. Be plucked up and planted far from me. Jesus said you would obey me, so do it in Jesus' name."

Someone said, "I can't forgive. I've tried, but I just can't do it. I can't forgive Brother So-and-so. You just don't know what he did to me."

No, I don't know what he did to you, but I know what unforgiveness will do to you. It will steal your faith, and possibly your life, if you don't talk to it and tell it where to go. Don't be overcome with evil, but overcome evil with good. (Rom. 12:21.)

5

Plant a Seed for What You Need

The Gospel according to Jesus says, "If you had faith as a seed, you wouldn't need more faith. You would simply plant the faith you have, and it would produce." You plant it by saying it. Any good farmer knows you plant a seed for what you need or desire. That seed is the substance of what you desire.

Faith as a Seed Causes You To Speak

Whatever you desire, you speak, based on the authority of God's Word. Jesus said it would obey you.

In Matthew 17:20 Jesus is explaining to His disciples why they couldn't cast the demon out of a boy.

And Jesus said unto them, Because of your unbelief: for verily I say unto you, If ye have faith as a grain of mustard seed, ye shall say unto this mountain, Remove hence to yonder place; and it shall remove; and nothing shall be impossible unto you.

Again, He is saying that if you have faith as a seed, you shall say.

It would be foolish for a farmer to buy seed, store it in a barn, pray for a harvest, and then at harvest time say, "I don't understand. I had faith. I had the seed, but I didn't get a harvest." Any farmer knows that seed produces only when it is planted.

It doesn't take great faith to produce a harvest. It doesn't take an acorn as big as a house to grow a huge oak tree; it only takes a small seed. The substance of that tree is in the acorn.

The substance of what you desire is in faith, and that comes from the Word of God. But faith is like a seed: if you don't plant it, it won't produce. It only develops to its full potential when planted.

Matthew 17:20 tells you how to plant the seed: "If you have faith as a seed, *you shall say unto the mountain.*" Jesus is talking about a mountain of adversity in your life.

This is a way to express your faith. If you have faith as a seed, you say to the mountain of adversity, "You're not going to hinder me. I take authority over you and cast you out. Financial lack, I'm talking to you. Leave my house. You can't stay."

The first time you say that, you may think, "Dear Lord, what am I saying? I must be losing my mind." Your carnal mind will try to come against your expression of faith.

If the Word of God is in you, you have faith. You know the Word is true; but if you haven't been voicing it, you haven't been planting it. Results always come after the Word is planted.

Having faith in the faith you already have is like a farmer who has faith in the seed he plants.

The Word says faith comes by hearing. You can hear me speaking the Word of God, and it will produce *some* faith in you. You can even have faith that it will work for someone else; but faith or confidence in your faith is developed by speaking God's Word yourself. You won't have faith in your faith by just hearing me tell you stories of how my faith worked for me. That's not enough. You must be fully persuaded in your own spirit.

Faith in the Substance

When you have faith in your faith, you have faith in the substance of things. You're not only planting a seed of faith, you're having faith in the seed you planted.

Jesus said, ...ye shall say unto this mountain, Remove hence to yonder place; and it shall remove.

Some say, "These people who talk to mountains and trees are just off in left field. I don't believe in talking to things." But follow them around a few days. You will find out what they really believe. You'll hear them say, "I heard on television that the plant is laying off workers. If you buy that new car, you'll be the first one laid off. Just watch and see."

What are they doing? Planting a seed of fear.

Has it happened? No.

Do they believe it's going to happen? Yes.

They're saying it. They believe; therefore, they speak. But they are only doing it on the negative side, not the positive. This is one of the laws of faith. The Apostle Paul quoted it.

> ...as it is written, I believed, and therefore have I spoken, we also believe, and therefore speak.

> —2 Corinthians 4:13

This is a spiritual law: What you believe, you speak.

Some say, "I already see that we will not be able to pay the note on the house that is due this fall, so we'll lose our house."

Where did they see that? As an image on the inside of them.

Good or Bad Seed Grows When Planted

When people say such things, they are planting seed. They will plant that seed day after day. Then they will fertilize it and water it. They have faith in their fears.

What are they doing? Calling something into existence. *They're actually calling things that are not as though they were,* but they are doing it on the negative side. The thing they fear will come upon them.

They talk to the mountain all the time and tell it how big it is and how fast it is growing. They talk to their car, curse it, and call it a "no-good wreck."

The more highly developed you get either in your fear or your faith, the quicker the manifestation will come.

Someone asked, "How long do I have to work on developing my faith?" Just until Jesus comes!

Faith comes easier for some than others. It depends on how you've been taught. If you've been taught a lot of religious unbelief, you will have to *unlearn some things.* Sometimes it's harder to unlearn than it is to learn, especially if you've been taught wrong.

Jesus said, "If you have faith as a seed, you *shall* say..." Not *maybe. You shall say.* So just check up on yourself and see if you have faith as a seed. Faith as a seed means faith that you are willing to plant.

Even though you have faith as a seed, that doesn't mean you are going to have a harvest tomorrow. It takes time for things to develop, so don't plant it today and plow it up tomorrow saying it didn't work.

Someone may say, "I have already said it twelve times. It's been eight days. It hasn't happened. It doesn't work for me."

All they are doing is working a formula. They don't have any faith in their faith. But if they keep saying what the Word of God said, it will produce faith in their seed. Then when it looks like it isn't working, they will dig around it, fertilize it, and continue in faith that the seed will produce.

6

Faith Without Results

In Acts 14 we find that Paul and Barnabas preached the gospel at Lystra, Derbe, Lycaonia, and the regions around them.

> And there sat a certain man at Lystra, impotent in his feet, being a cripple from his mother's womb, who never had walked:
>
> The same heard Paul speak: who stedfastly beholding him, and perceiving that he had faith to be healed,
>
> Said with a loud voice, Stand upright on thy feet. And he leaped and walked.
>
> —Acts 14:8-10

The Bible says he had faith to be healed, but he was not healed. Paul perceived this in his spirit.

Then I can imagine Paul asking himself, "If he had faith to be healed, why isn't he well?"

That man had not acted on his faith. It seems as though he didn't have faith in the faith that he had. Although he had faith to be healed, he was not healed. The Spirit of God revealed to Paul that the man was developed to the point that he was ready for the harvest.

Growing Stages

Remember, you don't plant a seed today and harvest it tomorrow. It develops in stages: first the blade, then the ear, then the full corn in the ear. If you try to harvest it too early, you will destroy the plant.

There is a time for planting and a time for harvest. *There has to be a time that you believe you receive.* You may not have the manifestation, but you know that the seed has been planted. The harvest is on the way. It's developing.

It could be that Paul came along at the time of harvest and sparked that man's faith into action. The Spirit of God revealed to Paul, "The man is ready for his harvest," so Paul said to him, "Stand upright on thy feet."

Faith Ignited by Boldness

The crippled man jumped up before he knew he couldn't do it. His faith was ignited by the boldness of Paul.

If someone had walked up to him and asked, "Do you believe that if we said a prayer over you and helped you up, you could walk?" the man would have said, "No. I haven't walked in all my life. I don't even know how."

However, Paul, perceiving that the man's faith was developed to the point of a harvest, just shouted at him, "Stand up on your feet!" and the man leaped and walked. But you don't take that as a formula. You can't say that's the way it will always work because not everyone is developed to the point of harvest.

Now let's look at this truth in reverse. There are people who are planting the seed of fear. By saying negative things over and over, they are becoming highly developed in their fears.

There will come a time when these negative things are developed to the point of harvest. Then they will happen quickly. And someone will always say, "I don't understand it. They were such good Christians. Why did God allow that to happen?" The answer is simple: they sowed and developed the wrong seed. *God will allow what we allow.*

As a farmer, it didn't take me long to learn that if I wanted a harvest of cotton, I didn't plant Johnson grass seed. I knew that everything produces after its kind. That's why I didn't have to plant it. The root was already there from the year before.

Have you noticed that you don't have to plant the bad seeds? You will have a harvest of weeds if you do nothing to control them.

That's what gets so many people in trouble. They say, "I'm just leaving it all up to God. Whatever the Lord wills for me to have will come my way." If you have ever raised a garden, you know that's not the thing to do.

If you turn your garden over to the Lord by saying, "Lord, whatever You will to grow in this garden, let it grow and I'll be satisfied," you will be disappointed with what grows in your garden. It will be *weeds, cockleburs,* and *Johnson grass* because the earth is under a curse and Satan is the god of this world.

Then you'll say, "I don't understand it. I really made a commitment to God." No, you committed your garden to the god of this world—the devil—and the curses came up.

It's our responsibility to sow the seed and develop our faith. Faith will work. It will not fail. *God's faith cannot fail. God's Word cannot fail;* it's incorruptible seed which can't be destroyed. *But what you do with the seed of the Word of God can cause it to fail to produce.* You can cause a production failure.

Faith in Your Seed

You could buy the best seeds in the world, plant them in the ground, then dig them up after two days, put them back in the sack, and say, "Seeds don't work."

You could take them back to the store and say, "I want my money back. These seeds don't know how to produce."

There was nothing wrong with the seed, *but you didn't have any faith in your seed.* If you have faith in the seed, you leave it planted. It will just keep eating on that mountain.

The devil may come to your carnal mind and tell you it's not working. It may look like it will never move that mountain. But it may be hollowing it out from the inside.

Some morning you will wake up to find that the mountain has collapsed. The Word of God and your faith ate it up from the inside. It still had the outer crust, but it was hollowed out. Then all of a sudden it collapsed.

7

Doers of the Word Are Confident

I want to share with you several things that will help you have faith in your faith. Being a doer of the Word is a good place to start.

> But be ye doers of the word, and not hearers only, deceiving your own selves.
>
> If any man among you seem to be religious, and bridleth not his tongue, but deceiveth his own heart, this man's religion is vain.
>
> —James 1:22,26

James says you deceive your own self if you are not a doer of the Word. Notice verse 26 says if you don't bridle your tongue, it will deceive your heart. So it is imperative that you keep God's Word in your heart.

This is where many Christians miss it in faith. They know the Word. They have the Word in them. Yet they have no faith in their ability to pray the prayer of faith because their heart condemns them.

Let's look at what Paul said in Romans, chapter 14:

> For meat destroy not the work of God. All things indeed are pure; but it is evil for that man who eateth with offence.
>
> It is good neither to eat flesh nor to drink wine, nor any thing whereby thy brother stumbleth, or is offended, or is made weak.
>
> Hast thou faith? have it to thyself before God. Happy is he that condemneth not himself in that thing which he alloweth.

—Romans 14:20-22

Paul is talking about eating meat offered to idols. He says, *Happy is the man who condemns not himself in that thing which he allows.* In other words, don't allow yourself to do things that will cause condemnation to come upon you.

And he that doubteth is damned if he eat, because he eateth not of faith: for whatsoever is not of faith is sin (v. 23).

There are certain things that you may not be able to do with a good conscience *because of the way you have been taught.* However, I could do those things with a good conscience because my mind has been renewed by the Word of God. It wouldn't affect my faith at all, but it would affect others' faith because they couldn't do it with a good conscience.

Paul is saying, "If something has been offered to idols, it doesn't mean anything because an idol is nothing." It wouldn't affect anything unless the person had been taught that it was wrong; then it would affect his conscience. The man who believes that it is wrong would be damned if he eats because he's not doing it in faith. His heart would condemn him.

So the bottom line is: Be a doer of God's Word, and don't do things that would condemn you.

Wrong Teaching—Wrong Believing

In the early days of the Pentecostal movement, men preached against radio and against automobiles. Years later one minister said, "I wish I hadn't preached so hard against those automobiles. I'd sure like to have one!" They preached against television, too, when it came out.

So the hearts of some would condemn them if they had a television set. To others it wouldn't affect their faith. But to them that are condemned, it would be wrong because it would violate their conscience.

This is what Paul is saying. You shouldn't do the things that condemn you.

Faith Worketh

In Galatians 5:6 Paul says:

For in Jesus Christ neither circumcision availeth any thing nor uncircumcision, but faith which worketh by love.

In other words, don't get so hung up on whether they've been circumcised or not, because it doesn't avail anything if they're in Christ. Faith worketh by love. Faith works; it's not lazy.

In a meeting one night I made this statement: "Don't get turned on to faith and say you'll quit your job and live by faith. You can live better by faith with a job than you can without one. If you can't live by faith with your job, you may starve without it."

A couple came to me after the service, and the man said, "Brother Capps, I'm glad we came tonight. I was going to quit my job tomorrow and live by faith."

Now you see, if God has called you into the full-time ministry, that would be a different situation. But we must use some common sense.

When Paul said faith works by love, he was talking about faith working in an atmosphere of love. If you're not walking in love, then you'll have no faith in your faith. I don't mean that just because you didn't walk in love, the Word of God is not still in you; but it is not producing.

A Truth, Not the Truth

Remember Paul said:

> So then faith cometh by hearing,
> and hearing by the word of God.

> —Romans 10:17

As I mentioned before, this is *a truth;* it is not *the whole truth.* Read what I am about to share with you very carefully, and don't misunderstand what I am saying. The Bible is *the* truth; but this Scripture passage is *a* truth—it is not the whole truth.

Don't ever take a truth and make it the whole truth. If you make that the absolute truth, then you would say faith couldn't come by any other means than by hearing the Word of God.

Romans 10:17 is specifically talking about faith in God and His Word. Faith in God comes by hearing what God said. Faith in me would come by hearing what I said. If I spoke what you knew to be fact, you would have faith in my word and in me by hearing what I said.

But if I were always saying something contrary to the Word of God, you would lose faith in me quickly.

Here is the point: Faith in God's Word comes from hearing the Word of God. Faith in the devil comes from hearing the words of the devil. The more you hear the words of the devil about negative things in life and things that come by the world's system, the more faith you will have in the devil's ability to keep you under the circumstances of life, for *faith cometh by hearing.*

Take Heed What You Hear

That's why it's necessary to fill your social life with people that believe and talk like you do: so your faith is not destroyed by their negativism. That is so important to your faith.

Jesus said, "Take heed what you hear." You must take heed what you hear, for *what you hear is what you will eventually believe* if you keep hearing it long enough.

There is a lot said today about balance, and I realize there must be balance. We also must use some common sense. Don't go beyond the Bible and say:

"I can have anything I say, so I'm going to have Brother So-and-so's wife."

Or, *"I need some money. I pray Brother So-and-so will lose his billfold and I will find it."*

As some have said, that's ignorance gone to seed! We shouldn't have to point out things like this, but we do because flaky people do flaky things.

A balance in faith is to stay with the Word of God.

When some people talk about balance in faith, they are talking about mixing faith and unbelief. That doesn't balance it; that neutralizes it. Then some will say, "Whatever happens must be the will of God, so who am I to resist it?" That's not balanced faith. That's dead faith! We are instructed to submit ourselves to God, resist the devil and he will flee from us. (James 4:7.)

Faith in God comes by hearing the Word of God.

Faith in the devil comes by hearing the words of the devil.

Faith in your faith comes by hearing your- self speak your faith.

Just as surely as faith in God's Word comes by hearing God's Word, hearing the words of the devil causes you to have faith in the devil and his ability. But if you keep hearing your voice speak God's Word in faith, it will cause you to have *faith in your own faith,* not just in others' faith.

Quoting the devil will destroy the faith you have in your faith. But if you will decree on the authority of God's Word what you believe, your faith will grow.

Some people believe things for which they have no basis in the Word of God. That's how they get out in left field in the area of faith. They believe things that they have no scriptural basis for. They just make up their own rules as they go.

But if you have the Word of God for what you believe, then you can quote and decree what you believe with confidence. As Paul said, ...*as it is written, I believed and therefore have I spoken...* (2 Cor. 4:13). He was quoting

David from Psalm 116:10. We believe and there-fore speak.

Whether you realize it or not, when you believe, you always speak. Sometimes you believe the wrong thing. That's the reason you speak the wrong thing, and why it is so impor-tant to choose carefully those with whom you continually associate. I don't mean shut your-self off from people, but choose those with whom you can talk faith. You can't afford to stay around and fellowship with unbelief. It will get on you. You will find yourself thinking, "I wonder if they're right," and wonder is the seed of doubt.

Someone said, "What about all the bad news on TV?"

It's okay to listen to the 10 o'clock news *if you will analyze it in light of the Word of God. But when you start analyzing the Word of God in light of the 10 o'clock news,* you're in trouble.

Fill your spirit with God's Word, and it will increase your faith in God's ability and willing-ness to deliver you from the fear of those things that are coming upon the earth.

8

Holding Faith and Good Conscience

This charge I commit unto thee, son Timothy, according to the prophecies which went before on thee, that thou by them mightest war a good warfare;

Holding faith, and a good conscience; which some having put away concerning faith have made shipwreck:

Of whom is Hymenaeus and Alexander; whom I have delivered unto Satan, that they may learn not to blaspheme.

—1 Timothy 1:18-20

Two times in Paul's ministry (that we have record of), he turned different individuals over to Satan for the destruction of the flesh that their spirit might be saved.

You can pray for people sometimes and keep the results of sin off of them. But when they knowingly walk in sin, refuse to repent, and rebel against what they know is right, there may come a time when you'll have to turn them over to the devil as Paul did. *But you must have the mind of Christ and the wisdom of God about when to do that.*

Notice Paul said, Holding faith, and a good conscience; which some having put away concerning faith have made shipwreck.

Remember, faith works by love. You can shipwreck your faith by walking out of love. That doesn't mean there's no faith in you. It simply means that the faith will not work without love.

You could have the same amount of the Word in you and walk out of love. The spiritual force of faith is there all right.

But you would have no faith in your faith because your heart condemns you for not walking in love.

When you get in strife, you open the door to the devil. Your faith is shut down because you have no confidence in it.

Paul gives us a key concerning faith when he says: Holding the mystery of the faith in a pure conscience (1 Tim. 3:9).

This is a key to the *mystery of the faith*. Paul is sharing with Timothy the mystery. This is why some people can't get their faith to work for them: they don't have a pure conscience.

Some Christians don't have a lack of faith, but they fail to have faith in the faith they do have. *If God's Word is inside them, they have faith. But it does not always produce for them.*

Known Sin Can Be a Factor

Sometimes people can't have faith in their faith because they are walking in known sin. If they are in known sin and praying for healing, they won't have any faith in their prayer because their heart condemns them because of the sin.

A raw sinner can get healed quicker than a Christian who is walking in known sin. You could call it a spiritual heart attack. Remember, Paul said, "Holding the mystery of faith in a pure conscience."

John says:

> For if our heart condemn us, God is greater than our heart, and knoweth all things.

> Beloved, if our heart condemn us not, then have we confidence toward God.

> And whatsoever we ask, we receive of him, because we keep his commandments, and do those things that are pleasing in his sight.

> —1 John 3:20-22

This is another factor that keeps people from having faith in the faith they have. Their heart condemns them, even if it is in little things. They don't have a pure conscience.

Jesus said, "I always do those things which please My Father." When you strive to always do the things that please God the Father, you will have great *faith in your faith.*

I challenge you to do everything within your ability to please your heavenly Father.

Oh, there will be times when you want to give someone a piece of your mind. But you know it wouldn't please the Father. Then it's time to make a decision. *You* have to make a decision to walk in love; no one can make it for you.

Love is not something you always feel like doing. You don't always feel like walking in love. *It's something you decide to do.* ...**God is love** (1 John 4:8); ...**God so loved the world, that he gave His** only begotten Son... (John 3:16).

Do you think God felt like having His Son killed? Do you think He had a good feeling about making His Son the sacrificial lamb for wicked people? You know He didn't, but He decided to do it because of love. He did it because He decided to love.

You can use your faith and love people, even when you don't want to. Some say, "But you don't know what they did to me." What they did to you won't compare with what they did to Jesus. God so loved that He gave His Son as the supreme sacrifice.

God decided to do it because of love. You can use your faith, and love the unlovely. That doesn't necessarily mean you are going to hug them around the neck every time you see them or have the same feeling for them as you have for your best friend. I'm talking about walking in love just because you decided to. In other words, you don't do things against them, and you don't talk against them; you love them just because it pleases the Father.

Keep His Commandments

And whatsoever we ask, we receive of him, because we keep his command-ments, and do those things that are pleasing in his sight.

—1 John 3:22

Notice the phrase, *and do those things that are pleasing in his sight.* If you just look at this on the surface, you'll think: "That means if you do good things, you'll build up credit with God. You'll get your prayers answered just because you do the good things."

If that is your thought, then you missed the whole point. The point John is making is that if you are going to have confidence or faith in

God to answer your prayers, then you must have *a pure conscience before God.* You don't get your prayers answered just because you do good things; but because you do the good things, you have a pure conscience before God and then your heart doesn't condemn you. By doing the things you know please the Father, that gives you a pure conscience.

If you said, "Well, I'm going to do it so I can get my prayers answered; I'm going to do this because God will have to answer my prayer," you're doing *right things* with *wrong motives.*

Do you know what Paul said about that kind of thinking?

For as many as are of the works of the law are under the curse... (Gal. 3:10). Under the Law people did good works, and that was counted to them for righteousness. *But today faith is counted for righteousness.* (Rom. 3:20-22.) Faith is the law of the New Covenant. (Rom. 3:26-31.)

Works was the law of the Old Covenant.

So when your heart condemns you, your faith is shut down. It will stop you from having faith in your faith.

9

Speaking in Agreement With God's Word

We've already seen in Romans 10:17 that faith in God and His Word comes by hearing God's Word. I believe, in the context of Romans 10, Paul reveals that *faith in your faith will come by hearing your own voice speaking and saying what you believe, based on the authority of God's Word.*

If you study what the Bible tells you about the God kind of faith, you will find that there is no release of the God kind of faith without words. That's the way it is released—through words.

Someone said, "What about people who can't speak?" Then they should write it down in faith. That would be their release of faith in words.

You release *your* faith in words. The God kind of faith is also released by speaking God's Word.

We see an example of this from the Old Testament, in the story of David and Goliath. When I was growing up, I learned about David and Goliath in Sunday school. All I learned was that David killed the giant. They made it look like God did it all, so I grew up thinking God was going to fight every battle for me. I was never taught the principles David used that brought the victory.

Here are some of the things that defeated the giant:

His Sword Was in His Mouth

And David spake to the men that stood by him, saying...who is this uncircumcised Philistine, that he should defy the armies of the living God?

And David said to Saul, Let no man's heart fail because of him; thy servant will go and fight with this Philistine.

And Saul said to David, Thou art not able to go against this Philistine to fight with him: for thou art but a youth, and he a man of war from his youth.

—1 Samuel 17:26,32-33

David said, "I'll go fight him."

Saul said, "Who do you think you are? You're just a youth. He's a man of war, trained from his youth. He's been in many battles. You can't go fight against him." Notice Saul didn't have any faith in David's faith. But here is his answer:

Thy servant slew both the lion and the bear: and this uncircumcised Philistine shall be as one of them, seeing he hath defied the armies of the living God.

David said moreover, The Lord that delivered me out of the paw of the lion, and out of the paw of the bear, he will deliver me out of the hand of this Philistine. And Saul said unto David, Go, and the Lord be with thee.

—1 Samuel 17:36-37

Not only did David have faith in his faith because of what he said, but his boldness in decreeing what he would do caused Saul to have faith in David's faith.

David *said* what he was going to do to that giant five times before he did it: "I'll take your head from your shoulders." *His confession was demonstrating faith in his faith.*

Some of you can think back and remember some things you have done in life for the simple reason that you started saying it. When you started saying it, you didn't think you would ever really do it; but you kept saying it until you started believing you could do it. Then you did it, and it seemed easy. Your words produced confidence in your faith, and you acted.

Words Produce Desire

I've always wanted to fly. My first flight was with a set of wings made out of shoebox lids when I was about four years old. It didn't last long. I had an inverted landing! But I kept saying, "I'm going to fly an airplane one of these days."

I didn't know what I was doing, but I put that desire in my heart by my words. Proverbs says it this way: ...when the desire cometh, it is a tree of life (Prov. 13:12). You can draw from that tree of life which is *desire.*

When desire hits you, you will start talking about it. I started saying, "I'm going to fly one of these days." When I tried flying off that barn, my wings didn't work very well; but they looked pretty good to a four-year-old boy with a great desire to fly.

I spoke words that set some cornerstones in my life and caused me to believe it. Eventually, it came to pass.

If you will think back a few years, there are places you've been and things you've done that you thought you never would do, but you started saying, "I'm going to do that one of these days."

Because there was a desire, you said it over and over until it got down inside you. Then you began to have faith in what you said, and your words increased your desire. That faith maneuvered you into the position to cause it to come to pass. But they didn't teach that to us in Sunday school.

A Sword in the Mouth Is Worth Two in a Sheath

David didn't just kill Goliath with the rock; he killed him with the *sword of his mouth.* He stood there in front of Goliath and said, "I'm going to take your head off your shoulder. I'll feed your carcass to the fowls of the air; not only you, but all the hosts of the Philistines."

That's a big statement for a 17-year-old boy who doesn't even have a sword. He's going to take the man's head off; but all he has is a rock, a sling—and faith in God.

David said it and said it and said it; then he did it. He didn't have a sword in his hand, *but he had one in his mouth*—the two-edged sword! David based what he said on his knowledge of God and His Word. He knew he had a covenant with God, and he had proven that covenant. So the giant was no match for him.

10

Don't Go Whole Hog When Half Ready

And in the fourth watch of the night Jesus went unto them, walking on the sea.

And when the disciples saw him walking on the sea, they were troubled, saying, It is a spirit; and they cried out for fear.

But straightway Jesus spake unto them, saying, Be of good cheer; it is I; be not afraid.

And Peter answered him and said, Lord, if it be thou, bid me come unto thee on the water.

And he said, Come. And when Peter was come down out of the ship, he walked on the water, to go to Jesus.

—Matthew 14:25-29

Here Peter has great faith in his faith. He says, "Lord, if it's You, bid me to come." Jesus answered with only one word, "Come."

As I was praying one day, I said: "Lord, I see a lot of people that go beyond their faith. They jump out of their boat when they're not ready to walk on the water. They get emotionally excited, and they jump out beyond where they are developed. I can see that Peter did that, and I would like to know why You called him out of the boat when he was not ready for water-walking faith."

The Lord said, "I didn't do it."

I said, "But You did."

Have you ever argued with the Lord? I knew I was right. I had read it a hundred times, but the Lord said, "Turn to it and read it."

I could hardly wait to read it to Him. "Right here in verse 29 You said, 'Come.'"

He said, "Read the preceding verse." So I did.

And Peter answered him and said, Lord, if it be thou, bid me come unto thee on the water (v. 28).

The Lord said to me, "What was I going to say: 'No, Peter, it's not Me?' All I did was answer his question."

Then I understood it for the first time. Peter didn't give Jesus any choice. He said, "If it's really You, bid me come." If Jesus had kept silent, He would have lied. If he had said, "No, Peter, don't come," it would have been a lie.

Jesus spoke one word, "Come." He simply answered Peter's question. I believe He intends for this to reveal more than what we have gotten out of it.

Sometimes we are like Peter; we paint ourselves into a corner. We say, "God, if You want me to do that, then let this happen." It was God's will for you to do that, but it wasn't God's will for this to happen.

Excited Faith

Peter said, "Bid me come." Jesus said, "Come." Peter got out of the boat and walked on the water to go to Jesus.

But when he saw the wind boisterous, he was afraid, and beginning to sink, he cried, saying Lord, save me.

—Matthew 14:30

Ask yourself this question: *What did the wind have to do with it?*

Peter saw the wind boisterous, and he was afraid.

The devil probably said, "Peter, did you notice how high the wind is?"

Let's think about this for a moment. What does the wind have to do with walking on water? Not a thing.

But the devil knows you must be single-minded if you're going to have faith in your faith.

This is how your faith slips away from you: when you begin to look at things that have nothing at all to do with what you're believing or what you're doing. In Peter's case it caused fear to come.

Peter began to give ear to the words of the enemy or his carnal mind. Many times we say the devil said something when it was our carnal mind. Our carnal mind is enmity against God and not subject to the law of God. (Rom. 8:7.) It must be renewed *by the Word* of God.

...and beginning to sink, he cried, saying Lord, save me (Matt. 14:30).

Notice the phrase, *beginning to sink*. Have you ever seen someone step into a swimming pool and *begin* to sink—first to his knees, then to his waist? No. He sank immediately, if not sooner.

But your faith doesn't leave you all at once. When Peter got his eyes on the circumstances, fear began to come and faith began to fade. This proves that you can have faith and lose it. Peter lost his faith slowly, and slowly he began to sink. He was taken by outward circumstances that had nothing to do with walking on water.

To walk by faith, you must be a noncon-formist. Paul said, ...be not conformed to this world, but be ye transformed by the renewing of your mind... (Rom. 12:2). You renew your mind to the Word of God. God's Word in you renews the mind.

11

Praying in the Spirit

When I call to remembrance the unfeigned faith that is in thee, which dwelt first in thy grandmother Lois and thy mother Eunice; and I am persuaded that in thee also.

Wherefore I put thee in remembrance that thou stir up the gift of God, which is in thee by the putting on of my hands.

—2 Timothy 1:5-6

In verse 5 Paul writes to young Timothy, reminding him of the faith that was in his grandmother Lois and his mother, Eunice. We know from Paul's writings in Romans 10:17 that faith comes by hearing, and hearing by the Word of God. Therefore this faith that is in Timothy was not inherited, although it was "handed down." The Word of God was taught by Lois to her daughter Eunice who then taught that Word to her son Timothy.

Next, in verse 6, Paul reminds Timothy to stir up the gift of God that is in him by the laying on of Paul's hands. Here Paul is not referring to faith. That is not the gift of God that Timothy received from Paul. Nowhere in the Bible does it say to lay hands on people to give them faith. Rather, the gift which Paul is telling Timothy to stir up is the gift of the Holy Spirit.

The Holy Ghost is the gift a person can receive by the laying on of hands. So Paul is telling Timothy, "Stir up the gift (the Holy Ghost) which you received when I laid hands on you."

Keep By the Holy Ghost

Hold fast the form of sound words, which thou hast heard of me, in faith and love which is in Christ Jesus.

That good thing which was committed unto thee keep by the Holy Ghost which dwelleth in us.

—2 Timothy 1:13-14

Hold fast sound words. Keep that good thing which was committed to you by the Holy Ghost.

What good thing? The unfeigned faith.

How do you keep it? By the gift of the Holy Ghost that was given by the laying on of hands.

Someone said, "What good is all that talking in tongues? Nobody can understand it." The Bible says you speak not unto men, but unto God. Ask yourself this: Would it be of any benefit to have a direct communication with God? Paul said it will build you up. It will edify you. Then Jude adds some light to the subject by saying:

> But ye, beloved, building up your-
> selves on your most holy faith, praying
> in the Holy Ghost,
>
> Keep yourselves in the love of
> God, looking for the mercy of our Lord
> Jesus Christ unto eternal life.
>
> —Jude 20-21

Praying in the Holy Ghost will build you up in your most holy faith. He didn't say it would give you faith. He didn't say that God would build you up. You build yourself up in your most holy faith by praying in the Holy Ghost.

God's Faith Is in His Word

When we are talking about having faith in God's Word and getting the Word of God in you, we are simply saying that if the Word of God abides within you, then you have the faith of God in you, because God's faith is in the Word.

In other words we get God's faith out of His Word because He filled His Word with faith. But Jude is talking about *our* faith. He's not talking about God's faith, but our own faith. In other words, that faith that you and I received from the Word of God becomes our individual faith. It is in us. It is ours to use. He tells us to build up *ourselves* on *our* most holy faith by *praying in the Holy Ghost*.

You could have faith inside you and still not accomplish one single thing—unless you have faith in the faith that is in you, faith enough to cause you to act.

You could have money, but if you didn't have faith that somebody would accept that money in exchange for groceries, you might starve to death with a purse or billfold full of cash. In order to benefit from all the money you have in your possession, you must have faith enough in that money to use it to buy the things you need.

It didn't take you long to figure out that in order to benefit from your money, you had to spend it. You learned that by experience. You have faith in money; you have no doubt that merchants all over the country will accept it in exchange for goods and services. That's why money is so important. You need it to get the things necessary for life.

The same thing is true of faith. One reason David was so strong in faith was because faith wasn't just a theory to David. He had already proven it in battles with a lion and a bear. He had proven his method—he knew it worked.

David refused to use another man's method or another's weapons.

They couldn't talk him out of his faith. He had great faith in *his method* because he had proven it.

For your situation, start where you are with your faith. Use it in the small things first. Develop yourself in it, then you will have great confidence in your faith. As your faith grows, so will your accomplishments.

There are two important things that Jude tells us praying in the Holy Ghost will do. *It will build you up in the faith that is inside you, and it will keep you in the love of God.*

These two benefits are very important for the development of our faith. Remember what Paul said in Galatians 5:6: ...**faith...worketh by love.** Without faith we have no power for successful life. Without the love of God in us, the faith we do have will not work for us.

If you are angry at someone who has offended you, begin to pray in the Holy Spirit and you won't stay angry long. Instead, your faith and your love will both grow.

12

Igniting Faith

And when there was an assault made both of the Gentiles, and also of the Jews with their rulers, to use them despitefully, and to stone them,

They were ware of it, and fled unto Lystra and Derbe, cities of Lycaonia, and unto the region that lieth round about:

And there they preached the gospel.

And there sat a certain man at Lystra, impotent in his feet, being a cripple from his mother's womb, who never had walked:

The same heard Paul speak: who stedfastly beholding him, and perceiving that he had faith to be healed,

Said with a loud voice, Stand upright
on thy feet. And he leaped and walked.

—Acts 14:5-10

When your faith is passive and you have
not acted on it, the boldness of another
person's faith can ignite the faith that you have.

This passage of Scripture from Acts 14 is a
classic example of this. Paul was preaching to
a group of people, including a man, crippled
from his mother's womb, who had never walked.
The Holy Ghost revealed to Paul that the man
had faith to be healed, but his faith had not yet
been released. This proves that you could have
faith to be healed and not be healed.

Paul said with a loud voice, **Stand upright
on thy feet.** And he leaped and walked. Notice
Paul didn't pray for him; he didn't lay hands on
him. You must realize that what happened had
something to do with that man's faith.

It also had something to do with Paul's faith.
Paul spoke with such boldness that it ignited
this fellow's faith and caused him to act on the
faith he already had.

In the ninth chapter of Acts, we find a similar incident.

> And it came to pass, as Peter passed throughout all quarters, he came down also to the saints which dwelt at Lydda.
>
> And there he found a certain man named Aeneas, which had kept his bed eight years, and was sick of the palsy.
>
> And Peter said unto him, Aeneas, Jesus Christ maketh thee whole: arise, and make thy bed. And he arose immediately.
>
> And all that dwelt at Lydda and Saron saw him, and turned to the Lord.
>
> —Acts 9:32-35

Notice that Peter came to the believers who dwelt at Lydda, not to the unbelievers. Aeneas was one of these believers. He had been bedfast for eight years, sick of the palsy.

Did you notice that Peter didn't pray for him? He didn't lay hands on him. Evidently this saint had the Word of God in him. He had faith, but it had not brought healing.

Peter said to him, "Aeneas, Jesus Christ makes you whole. Arise and make your bed." And he arose immediately!

Now remember, this man had been bedridden for eight years. Everyone who came along probably said, "Bless your heart; it will be worth it all one of these days. In the sweet by-and-by when you get to heaven, you will be well." But Peter approached him differently.

Allow me to paraphrase it. Peter said, "Aeneas, don't you know Jesus Christ maketh you whole? Get up! Make up your bed."

I can almost hear Aeneas saying, "Yeah, that's right. Jesus did make me whole, didn't He?" Then he just gathers up his bed and goes home.

What happened? The boldness of Peter's faith sparked the faith that was in Aeneas. In so many words, Peter said, "Hey, don't you know Jesus Christ has already done it all? Make up your bed!" Peter's boldness of faith ignited the faith in Aeneas, and he got up before he knew he couldn't.

The Church, the Body of Christ, doesn't have a problem with having faith in God, but they do have a problem having faith in their faith.

Have you noticed it in your life? There are times when you do something that you shouldn't or fail to spend as much time in the Word as you should. Then you begin to feel condemned.

For if our heart condemn us, God is greater than our heart, and knoweth all things.

Beloved, if our heart condemn us not, then have we confidence toward God.

—1 John 3:20-21

If your heart condemns you, the devil will get on your case and ride you into the ground if you let him. Condemnation is a tool the devil will use against you.

The Holy Spirit will convince or convict you. When He does, repent. But remember, Paul said:

There is therefore now no condemnation to them which are in Christ Jesus, who walk not after the flesh, but after the Spirit.

For the law of the Spirit of life in Christ Jesus hath made me free from the law of sin and death.

For what the law could not do, in
that it was weak through the flesh,
God sending his own Son in the likeness
of sinful flesh, and for sin, condemned
sin in the flesh.

—Romans 8:1-3

After the New Covenant is in effect, there is
no condemnation. If you are born again and
doing your best to please the Father in all that
you do, don't let that condemnation come against
you. It is a design of the devil to stop your faith.
Acting on 1 John 1:9 will destroy all condemnation and bring the peace of God.

Make a decision to spend time fellowship-
ping with your heavenly Father daily. Develop
a strong relationship with Him through prayer,
and with your Savior, Jesus, and the Holy
Ghost through the study and meditation of
God's Word daily.

Then you will find that faith in your faith will
grow exceedingly.

Charles Capps a farmer from England, Arkansas became an internationally known Bible teacher by sharing practical truths from the Word of God. His simplistic, down to earth  style of applying spiritual principles to daily life has appealed to people from every Christian denomination.

The requests for speaking engagements became so great after the printing of *God's Creative Power® Will Work for You* that he retired from farming and became a full-time Bible teacher. His books are available in multiple languages throughout the world.

Besides publishing 24 books, including best-sellers *The Tongue A Creative Force* and *God's Creative Power®* series which has sold over 6 million copies, Capps Ministries has a national daily radio broadcast and weekly TV broadcast called "Concepts of Faith".

For a complete list of CDs, DVDs, and books by
Charles Capps, or to receive his
publication, Concepts of Faith, write:

Charles Capps Ministries
P.O. Box 69, England, Arkansas 72046
Toll Free Order Line (24 hours)
1-877-396-9400
www.charlescapps.com

BOOKS BY CHARLES CAPPS
AND ANNETTE CAPPS

Angels

God's Creative Power® for Finances

God's Creative Power® - Gift Edition
(Also available in Spanish)

BOOKS BY ANNETTE CAPPS

Quantum Faith®

*Reverse The Curse in
Your Body and Emotions*

Overcoming Persecution

BOOKS BY CHARLES CAPPS

NEW RELEASE!-Calling Things That Are Not
Triumph Over The Enemy
When Jesus Prays Through You
The Tongue – A Creative Force
Releasing the Ability of God Through Prayer
End Time Events
Your Spiritual Authority
Changing the Seen and Shaping The Unseen
Faith That Will Not Change
Faith and Confession
God's Creative Power® Will Work For You
(Also available in Spanish)

God's Creative Power® For Healing
(Also available in Spanish)

Success Motivation Through the Word

God's Image of You

Seedtime and Harvest
(Also available in Spanish)

The Thermostat of Hope
(Also available in Spanish under the title
Hope- A Partner to Faith)

How You Can Avoid Tragedy

Kicking Over Sacred Cows

The Substance of Things
The Light of Life in the Spirit of Man
Faith That Will Work For You

Powerful Teaching From Charles Capps

If you have enjoyed reading this book, you can find more dynamic teaching from Charles Capps in these revolutionary books.

Can Your Faith Fail?

Faith That Will Not Change

Have you ever stepped out in faith only to later feel that you have failed? If you are like most Christians, at some point in your life, you have questioned the word God gave you.

The truth, however, is that faith is a law and God's laws always work. This is a practical guide to encourage you in your walk with God. It will teach you how to put your faith into action to produce results in your life.

ISBN-13: 978-0-9819574-6-3

You Can Change The Direction of Your Life

How You Can Avoid Tragedy And Live A Better Life

How often have you heard the question: "They were such good Christians! Why did this happen to them?" Many believers' lives have been overwhelmed needlessly by defeat and tragedy.

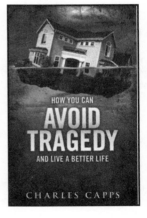

Satan's greatest weapon has been deception - getting you to believe something contrary to God's Word. Wrong speaking, wrong praying, and wrong believing will destroy your faith.

Praying "If it be Thy Will," has opened doors for the devil's opportunity when God's Will is already revealed in His Word.

ISBN-13: 978-0-9819574-5-6

Understanding Paul's "Thorn In The Flesh" And How You Can Overcome The Messenger Of Satan Assigned To You

Triumph Over The Enemy

In Second Corinthians 12:7, Paul writes about "a thorn in the flesh, the messenger of Satan" who had been sent to harass him. This "messenger" was sent to create problems and stir up the people against Paul everywhere he preached. But Paul knew the key to overcoming this obstacle – he learned to exercise his God-given authority here on the earth!

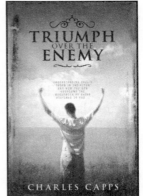

This book will show you how to walk in God's grace and triumph over this enemy sent to harass and keep you from God's greater blessings in your life.

ISBN-13: 978-0-9819574-2-5

Supernatural Deliverance
Is Available To You!

Angels
Knowing Their Purpose
Releasing Their Power

Angels want to be involved in every area of your life: in your home, your business, your finances and your family. These supernatural beings of God are just waiting for you to speak God's Word.

This book takes you on a fascinating journey of angelic intervention in Bible times and in the lives of the authors, Charles Capps and Annette Capps.

The ministry of angels is part of the salvation that God has given and a valid ministry in the earth today. Discover how the supernatural deliverance of angels can start changing your life!

ISBN-13: 978-0-9819574-1-8

Words Are The Most Powerful Things In The Universe!

The Tongue – A Creative Force

The words you speak will either put you over in life or hold you in bondage. Put yourself in a position to receive God's best for you by speaking His Word. God's creative power is still just as it was in the beginning of time, when He stood there and said, "Light-be," and light was. Man was created in the image of God and His likeness. His Word spoken from your mouth and conceived in your heart becomes a spiritual force releasing His ability within you.

I have told my people they can have what they say, but my people are saying what they have.

ISBN-13: 978-0-9820320-5-3

Uncover God's System for Answered Prayer

Releasing the Ability of God Through Prayer

God's Word is alive and powerful! It is living substance. It is law in the world of the spirit. Prayer is governed by spiritual laws and is designed to work for you. When

you learn to pray in line with Gods' Word, you release the ability of God and bring Him on the scene in your behalf. Discover the power of prayer that is governed by spiritual laws and designed to work for you. It is more powerful than the laws of nature that rule the universe today.

ISBN-13: 978-0-9820320-2-2

Seedtime and Harvest

God's Word is incorruptible seed, and God's promises are seeds for harvest. In this book you will learn that as you speak God's promises out of your mouth as a seed, it goes into your heart to grow and produce a harvest of blessing.

ISBN-13: 978-0-9819574-3-2

The Thermostat of HOPE

Surely no one would be foolish enough in natural things to argue with you when you turn the thermostat to 70 degrees, but they will when you set your goal on God's promises.

Hope, like a thermostat, is simply a goal-setter with no substance. Faith, which comes from the heart, is the substance of what you desire.

The heart (spirit) of man is like the heart of the heating-cooling unit. Designed by God to produce the very thing you plant in it. You plant it or set the goal by speaking it!

ISBN-13: 978-1-937578-30-5

New Release!!!

Calling Things That Are Not

The Powerful Realm of the Unseen

The principle of calling things that are not as though they were is the spiritual principle through which everything physical becomes manifest. God created light by calling for "light" when only darkness was there. Jesus used this same method,

call the lepers clean, and the dead to life, and peace to the storm.

You must call for what you desire. If you want your dog to come, you call the dog. You call for what is not there. Whatever you call in the natural will come. Call what does not exist and continue to call until it manifests.

ISBN 13: 978-1-937578-31-2